I0493946

This informational booklet provides a generic, non-exhaustive overview of OSHA standards-related topics. This publication does not itself alter or determine compliance responsibilities, which are set forth in OSHA standards themselves and the Occupational Safety and Health Act. Moreover, because interpretations and enforcement policy may change over time, for additional guidance on OSHA compliance requirements, the reader should consult current administrative interpretations and decisions by the Occupational Safety and Health Review Commission and the courts.

Material contained in this publication is in the public domain and may be reproduced, fully or partially, without permission of the Federal Government. Source credit is requested but not required.

This information will be made available to sensory impaired individuals upon request.
Voice phone: (202) 219-8045;
Telecommunications Device for the Deaf (TDD) message referral phone: 1-800-326-2577

Process Safety Management Guidelines for Compliance

U.S. Department of Labor
Robert B. Reich, Secretary

Occupational Safety and Health Administration
Joseph A. Dear, Assistant Secretary

OSHA 3133
1994 (Reprinted)

Contents

Illustrations

Purpose

The major objective of process safety management (PSM) of highly hazardous chemicals is to prevent unwanted releases of hazardous chemicals especially into locations that could expose employees and others to serious hazards. An effective process safety management program requires a systematic approach to evaluating the whole chemical process. Using this approach, the process design, process technology, process changes, operational and maintenance activities and procedures, nonroutine activities and procedures, emergency preparedness plans and procedures, training programs, and other elements that affect the process are all considered in the evaluation.

Application

The various lines of defense that have been incorporated into the design and operation of the process to prevent or mitigate the release of hazardous chemicals need to be evaluated and strengthened to ensure their effectiveness at each level. Process safety management is the proactive identification, evaluation and mitigation or prevention of chemical releases that could occur as a result of failures in processes, procedures, or equipment.

The process safety management standard targets highly hazardous chemicals that have the potential to cause a catastrophic incident. The purpose of the standard as a whole is to aid employers in their efforts to prevent or mitigate episodic chemical releases that could lead to a catastrophe in the workplace and possibly in the surrounding community.

To control these types of hazards, employers need to develop the necessary expertise, experience, judgement, and initiative within their work force to properly implement and maintain an effective process safety management program as envisioned in the Occupational Safety and Health Administration (OSHA) standard.

The OSHA standard is required by the Clean Air Act Amendments, as is the Environmental Protection Agency's Risk Management Plan, which will be proposed in 1992. Employers who merge the two sets of requirements into their process safety management program will better assure full compliance with each as well as enhance their relationship with the local community.

Although OSHA believes process safety management will have a positive effect on the safety of employees and will offer other potential benefits to employers, such as increased productivity, smaller businesses that may have limited resources available to them at this time, might consider alternative avenues of decreasing the risks associated with highly hazardous chemicals at their workplaces. One method that might be considered is reducing inventory of the highly hazardous chemical. This reduction in inventory will result in reducing the risk or potential for a catastrophic incident. Also, employers, including small employers, may establish more efficient inventory control by reducing, to below the established threshold, the quantities of highly hazardous chemicals onsite. This reduction can be accomplished by ordering smaller shipments and maintaining the minimum inventory necessary for efficient and safe operation. When reduced inventory is not feasible, the employer might consider dispersing inventory to several locations onsite. Dispersing storage into locations so that a release in one location will not cause a release in another location is also a practical way to reduce the risk or potential for catastrophic incidents.

Exceptions

The PSM standard does not apply to the following:

• Retail facilities;

• Oil or gas well drilling or servicing operations;

• Normally unoccupied remote facilities;

• Hydrocarbon fuels used solely for workplace consumption as a fuel (e.g., propane used for comfort heating, gasoline for vehicle refueling), if such fuels are not a part of a process containing another highly hazardous chemical covered by this standard; or

• Flammable liquids stored in atmospheric tanks or transferred, which are kept below their normal boiling point without benefit of chilling or refrigerating and are not connected to a process.

Process Safety Information

Hazards of the Chemicals Used in the Process

Complete and accurate written information concerning process chemicals, process technology, and process equipment is essential to an effective process safety management program and to a process hazard analysis. The compiled information will be a necessary resource to a variety of users including the team performing the process hazard analysis as required by PSM; those developing the training programs and the operating procedures; contractors whose employees will be working with the process; those conducting the pre-startup reviews; as well as local emergency preparedness planners, and insurance and enforcement officials.

The information to be compiled about the chemicals, including process intermediates, needs to be comprehensive enough for an accurate assessment of the fire and explosion characteristics, reactivity hazards, the safety and health hazards to workers, and the corrosion and erosion effects on the process equipment and monitoring tools. Current material safety data sheet (MSDS) information can be used to help meet this requirement but must be supplemented with process chemistry information, including runaway reaction and over-pressure hazards, if applicable.

Technology of the Process

Process technology information will be a part of the process safety information package and should include employer-established criteria for maximum inventory levels for process chemicals; limits beyond which would be considered upset conditions; and a qualitative estimate of the consequences or results of deviation that could occur if operating beyond the established process limits. Employers are encouraged to use diagrams that will help users understand the process.

A block flow diagram is used to show the major process equipment and interconnecting process flow lines and flow rates, stream composition, temperatures, and pressures when necessary for clarity. The block flow diagram is a simplified diagram.

Process flow diagrams are more complex and show all main flow streams including valves to enhance the understanding of the process as well as pressures and temperatures on all feed and product lines within all major vessels and in and out of headers and heat exchangers, and points of pressure and temperature control (see Figure 1 for a sample process flow diagram). Also, information on construction materials, pump capacities and pressure heads, compressor horsepower, and vessel design pressures and temperatures are shown when necessary for clarity. In addition, process flow diagrams usually show major components of control loops along with key utilities.

Figure 1

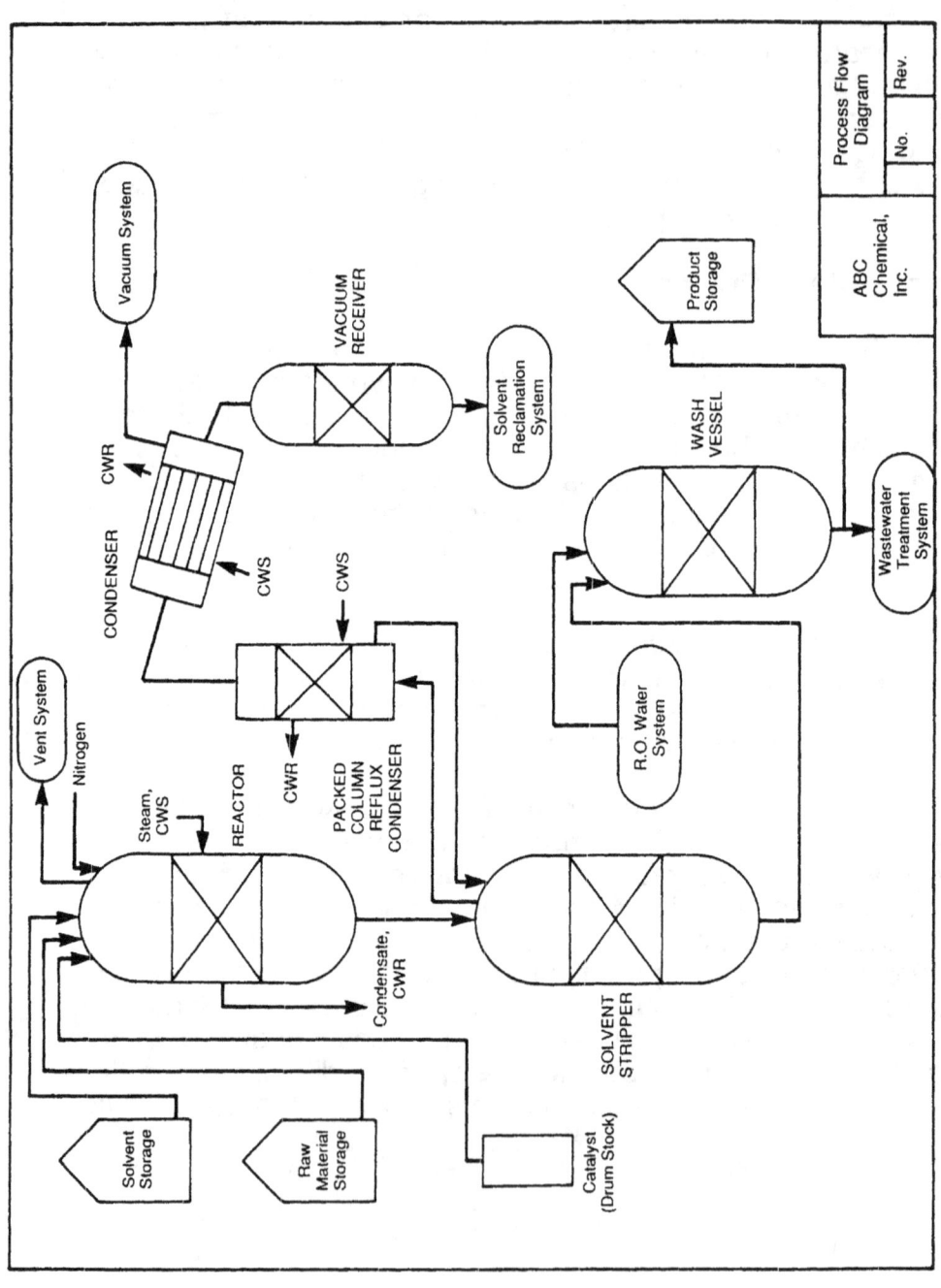

Equipment in the Process

Piping and instrument diagrams (P&IDs) may be the more appropriate type diagrams to show some of the above details as well as display the information for the piping designer and engineering staff. The P&IDs are to be used to describe the relationships between equipment and instrumentation as well as other relevant information that will enhance clarity. Computer software programs that do P&IDs or other diagrams useful to the information package may be used to help meet this requirement.

The information pertaining to process equipment design must be documented. In other words, what codes and standards were relied on to establish good engineering practice? These codes and standards are published by such organizations as the American Society of Mechanical Engineers, the American Petroleum Institute, American National Standards Institute, National Fire Protection Association, American Society for Testing and Materials, The National Board of Boiler and Pressure Vessel Inspectors, National Association of Corrosion Engineers, American Society of Exchange Manufacturers Association, and Model Building Code groups.

For existing equipment designed and constructed many years ago in accordance with the codes and standards available at that time and no longer in general use today, the employer must document which codes and standards were used and that the design and construction along with the testing, inspection, and operation are still suitable for the intended use. Where the process technology requires a design that departs from the applicable codes and standards, the employer must document that the design and construction are suitable for the intended purpose.

Employee Involvement

Section 304 of the Clean Air Act Amendments states that employers are to consult with their employees and their representatives regarding their efforts in developing and implementing the process safety management program elements and hazard assessments. Section 304 also requires employers to train and educate their employees and to inform affected employees of the findings from incident investigations required by the process safety management program. Many employers, under their existing safety and health programs, already have established methods to keep employees and their representatives informed about relevant safety and health issues and may be able to adapt these practices and procedures to meet their obligations under PSM.

Employers who have not implemented an occupational safety and health program may wish to form a safety and health committee of employees and management representatives to help the employer meet the PSM obligations. Such a committee can be a significant ally in helping the employer implement and maintain an effective process safety management program for all employees.

Process Hazard Analysis

A process hazard analysis (PHA), or evaluation, is one of the most important elements of the process safety management program. A PHA is an organized and systematic effort to identify and analyze the significance of potential hazards associated with the processing or handling of highly hazardous chemicals. A PHA provides information that will assist employers and employees in making decisions for improving safety and reducing the consequences of unwanted or unplanned releases of hazardous chemicals.

A PHA analyzes potential causes and consequences of fires, explosions, releases of toxic or flammable chemicals, and major spills of hazardous chemicals. The PHA focuses on equipment, instrumentation, utilities, human actions (routine and nonroutine), and external factors that might affect the process.

The selection of a PHA methodology or technique will be influenced by many factors including how much is known about the process. Is it a process that has been operated for a long period of time with little or no innovation and extensive experience has been generated with its use? Or, is it a new process or one that has been changed frequently by the inclusion of innovation features? Also, the size and complexity of the process will influence the decision as to the appropriate PHA methodology to use. All PHA methodologies are subject to certain limitations. For example, the checklist methodology works well when the process is very stable and no changes are made, but it is not as effective when the process has undergone extensive change. The checklist may miss the most recent changes and consequently they would not be evaluated. Another limitation to be considered concerns the assumptions made by the team or analyst. The PHA is dependent on good judgement and the assumptions made during the study need to be documented and understood by the team and reviewer and kept for a future PHA.

The team conducting the PHA needs to understand the methodology that is going to be used. A PHA team can vary in size from two people to a number of people with varied operational and technical backgrounds. Some team members may be part of the team for only a limited time. The team leader needs to be fully knowledgeable in the proper implementation of the PHA methodology to be used and should be impartial in the evaluation. The other full or part-time team members need to provide the team with expertise in areas such as process technology; process design; operating procedures and practices; alarms; emergency procedures; instrumentation; maintenance procedures, both routine and nonroutine tasks, including how the tasks are authorized; procurement of parts and supplies; safety and health; and any other relevant subjects. At least one team member must be familiar with the process.

The ideal team will have an intimate knowledge of the standards, codes, specifications, and regulations applicable to the process being studied. The selected team members need to be compatible and the team leader needs to be able to manage the team and the PHA study. The team needs to be able to work together while benefiting from the expertise of others on the team or outside the team to resolve issues and to forge a consensus on the findings of the study and recommendations.

The application of a PHA to a process may involve the use of different methodologies for various parts of the process. For example, a process involving a series of unit operations of varying sizes, complexities, and ages may use different methodologies and team members for each operation. Then the conclusions can be integrated into one final study and evaluation.

A more specific example is the use of a PHA checklist for a standard boiler or heat exchanger and the use of a Hazard and Operability PHA for the overall process. Also, for batch-type processes like custom batch operations, a generic PHA of a representative batch may be used where there are only small changes of monomer or other ingredient ratio and the chemistry is documented for the full range and ratio of batch ingredients. Another process where the employer might consider using a generic type of PHA is a gas plant. Often these plants are simply moved from site to site, and therefore, a generic PHA may be used for these movable plants. Also, when an employer has several similar size gas plants and no sour gas is being processed at the site, a generic PHA is feasible as long as the variations of the individual sites are accounted for in the PHA.

Finally, when an employer has a large continuous process with several control rooms for different portions of the process, such as for a distillation tower and a blending operation, the employer may wish to do each segment separately and then integrate the final results.

Small businesses covered by this rule often will have processes that have less storage volume and less capacity and may be less complicated than processes at a large facility. Therefore, OSHA would anticipate that the less complex methodologies would be used to meet the process hazard analysis criteria in the standard. These process hazard analyses can be done in less time and with fewer people being involved. A less complex process generally means that less data, P&IDs, and process information are needed to perform a process hazard analysis.

Many small businesses have processes that are not unique, such as refrigerated warehouses or cold storage lockers or water treatment facilities. Where employer associations have a number of members with such facilities, a generic PHA, evolved from a checklist or what-if questions, could be developed and effectively used by employers to reflect their particular process; this would simplify compliance for them.

When the employer has a number of processes that require a PHA, the employer must set up a priority system to determine which PHAs to conduct first. A preliminary hazard analysis may be useful in setting priorities for the processes that the employer has determined are subject to coverage by the process safety management standard. Consideration should be given first to those processes with the potential of adversely affecting the largest number of employees. This priority setting also should consider the potential severity of a chemical release, the number of potentially affected employees, the operating history of the process, such as the frequency of chemical releases, the age of the process, and any other relevant factors. Together, these factors would suggest a ranking order using either a weighting factor system or a systematic ranking method. The use of a preliminary hazard analysis will assist an employer in determining which process should be of the highest priority for hazard analysis resulting in the greatest improvement in safety at the facility occurring first.

Detailed guidance on the content and application of process hazard analysis methodologies is available from the American Institute of Chemical Engineers' Center for Chemical Process Safety, 345 E. 47th Street, New York, New York 10017, (212) 705-7319. Also, see the discussion of various methods of process hazard analysis contained in the Appendix to this publication.

Operating Procedures

Operating procedures describe tasks to be performed, data to be recorded, operating conditions to be maintained, samples to be collected, and safety and health precautions to be taken. The procedures need to be technically accurate, understandable to employees, and revised periodically to ensure that they reflect current operations. The process safety information package helps to ensure that the operating procedures and practices are consistent with the known hazards of the chemicals in the process and that the operating parameters are correct. Operating procedures should be reviewed by engineering staff and operating personnel to ensure their accuracy and that they provide practical instructions on how to actually carry out job duties safely. Also the employer must certify annually that the operating procedures are current and accurate.

Operating procedures provide specific instructions or details on what steps are to be taken or followed in carrying out the stated procedures. The specific instructions should include the applicable safety precautions and appropriate information on safety implications. For example, the operating procedures addressing operating parameters will contain operating instructions about pressure limits, temperature ranges, flow rates, what to do when an upset condition occurs, what alarms and instruments are pertinent if an upset condition occurs, and other subjects. Another example of using operating instructions to properly implement operating procedures is in starting up or shutting down the process. In these cases, different parameters will be required from those of normal operation. These operating instructions need to clearly indicate the distinctions between startup and normal operations, such as the appropriate allowances for heating up a unit to reach the normal operating parameters. Also, the operating instructions need to describe the proper method for increasing the temperature of the unit until the normal operating temperatures are reached.

Computerized process control systems add complexity to operating instructions. These operating instructions need to describe the logic of the software as well as the relationship between the equipment and the control system; otherwise, it may not be apparent to the operator.

Operating procedures and instructions are important for training operating personnel. The operating procedures are often viewed as the standard operating practices (SOPs) for operations. Control room personnel and operating staff, in general, need to have a full understanding of operating procedures. If workers are not fluent in English, then procedures and instructions need to be prepared in a second language understood by the workers. In addition, operating procedures need to be changed when there is a change in the process. The consequences of operating procedure changes need to be fully evaluated and the information conveyed to the personnel. For example, mechanical changes to the process made by the maintenance department (like changing a valve from steel to brass or other subtle changes) need to be evaluated to determine whether operating procedures and practices also need to be changed. All management of change actions must be coordinated and integrated with current operating procedures, and operating personnel must be alerted to the changes in procedures before the change is made. When the process is shut down to make a change, then the operating procedures must be updated before re-starting the process.

Training must include instruction on how to handle upset conditions as well as what operating personnel are to do in emergencies such as pump seal failures or pipeline ruptures. Communication among operating personnel and workers within the process area performing nonroutine tasks also must be maintained. The hazards of the tasks are to be conveyed to operating personnel in accordance with established procedures and to those performing the actual tasks. When the work is completed, operating personnel should be informed to provide closure on the job.

Employee Training

All employees, including maintenance and contractor employees involved with highly hazardous chemicals, need to fully understand the safety and health hazards of the chemicals and processes they work with so they can protect themselves, their fellow employees, and the citizens of nearby communities. Training conducted in compliance with the OSHA Hazard Communication standard (*Title 29 Code of Federal Regulations* (CFR) Part 1910.1200) will inform employees about the chemicals they work with and familiarize them with reading and understanding MSDSs. However, additional training in subjects such as operating procedures and safe work practices, emergency evacuation and response, safety procedures, routine and nonroutine work authorization activities, and other areas pertinent to process safety and health need to be covered by the employer's training program.

In establishing their training programs, employers must clearly identify the employees to be trained, the subjects to be covered, and the goals and objectives they wish to achieve. The learning goals or objectives should be written in clear measurable terms before the training begins. These goals and objectives need to be tailored to each of the specific training modules or segments. Employers should describe the important actions and conditions under which the employee will demonstrate competence or knowledge as well as what is acceptable performance.

Hands-on training, where employees actually apply lessons learned in simulated or real situations, will enhance learning. For example, operating personnel, who will work in a control room or at control panels, would benefit by being trained at a simulated control panel. Upset conditions of various types could be displayed on the simulator, and then the employee could go through the proper operating procedures to bring the simulator panel back to the normal operating parameters. A training environment could be created to help the trainee feel the full reality of the situation but under controlled conditions. This type of realistic training can be very effective in teaching employees correct procedures while allowing them also to see the consequences of what might happen if they do not follow established operating procedures. Other training techniques using videos or training also can be very effective for teaching other job tasks, duties, or imparting other important information. An effective training program will allow employees to fully participate in the training process and to practice their skills or knowledge.

Employers need to evaluate periodically their training programs to see if the necessary skills, knowledge, and routines are being properly understood and implemented by their trained employees. The methods for evaluating the training should be developed along with the training program goals and objectives. Training program evaluation will help employers to determine the amount of training their employees understood and whether the desired results were obtained. If, after the evaluation, it appears that the trained employees are not at the level of knowledge and skill that was expected, the employer should revise the training program, provide retraining, or provide more frequent refresher training sessions until the deficiency is resolved. Those who conducted the training and those who received the training also should be consulted as to how best to improve the training process. If there is a language barrier, the language known to the trainees should be used to reinforce the training messages and information.

Careful consideration must be given to ensure that employees, including maintenance and contract employees, receive current and updated training. For example, if changes are made to a process, affected employees must be trained in the changes and understand the effects of the changes on their job tasks. Additionally, as already discussed, the evaluation of the employee's absorption of training will certainly determine the need for further training.

Contractors

Employers who use contractors to perform work in and around processes that involve highly hazardous chemicals have to establish a screening process so that they hire and use only contractors who accomplish the desired job tasks without compromising the safety and health of any employees at a facility. For contractors whose safety performance on the job is not known to the hiring employer, the employer must obtain information on injury and illness rates and experience and should obtain contractor references. In addition, the employer must ensure that the contractor has the appropriate job skills, knowledge, and certifications (e.g., for pressure vessel welders). Contractor work methods and experience should be evaluated. For example, does the contractor conducting demolition work swing loads over operating processes or does the contractor avoid such hazards?

Maintaining a site injury and illness log for contractors is another method employers must use to track and maintain current knowledge of activities involving contract employees working on or adjacent to processes covered by PSM. Injury and illness logs of both the employer's employees and contract employees allow the employer to have full knowledge of process injury and illness experience. This log contains information useful to those auditing process safety management compliance and those involved in incident investigations.

Contract employees must perform their work safely. Considering that contractors often perform very specialized and potentially hazardous tasks, such as confined space entry activities and nonroutine repair activities, their work must be controlled while they are on or near a process covered by PSM. A permit system or work authorization system for these activities is helpful for all affected employers. The use of a work authorization system keeps an employer informed of contract employee activities. Thus, the employer has better coordination and more management control over the work being performed in the process area. A well-run and well-maintained process, where employee safety is fully recognized, benefits all of those who work in the facility whether they are employees of the employer or the contractor.

Pre-Startup Safety Review

For new processes, the employer will find a PHA helpful in improving the design and construction of the process from a reliability and quality point of view. The safe operation of the new process is enhanced by making use of the PHA recommendations before final installations are completed. P&IDs should be completed, the operating procedures put in place, and the operating staff trained to run the process, before startup. The initial startup procedures and normal operating procedures must be fully evaluated as part of the pre-startup review to ensure a safe transfer into the normal operating mode.

For existing processes that have been shutdown for turnaround or modification, the employer must ensure that any changes other than "replacement in kind" made to the process during shutdown go through the management of change procedures. P&IDs will need to be updated, as necessary, as well as operating procedures and instructions. If the changes made to the process during shutdown are significant and affect the training program, then operating personnel as well as employees engaged in routine and nonroutine work in the process area may need some refresher or additional training. Any incident investigation recommendations, compliance audits, or PHA recommendations need to be reviewed to see what affect they may have on the process before beginning the startup.

Mechanical Integrity of Equipment

Employers must review their maintenance programs and schedules to see if there are areas where "breakdown" maintenance is used rather than the more preferable on-going mechanical integrity program. Equipment used to process, store, or handle highly hazardous chemicals has to be designed, constructed, installed, and maintained to minimize the risk of releases of such chemicals. This requires that a mechanical integrity program be in place to ensure the continued integrity of process equipment.

Elements of a mechanical integrity program include identifying and categorizing equipment and instrumentation, inspections and tests and their frequency; maintenance procedures; training of mainte-nance personnel; criteria for acceptable test results; documentation of test and inspection results; and documentation of manufacturer recommendations for equipment and instrumentation.

Process Defenses

The first line of defense an employer has is to operate and maintain the process as designed and to contain the chemicals. This is backed up by the second line of defense which is to control the release of chemicals through venting to scrubbers or flares, or to surge or overflow tanks designed to receive such chemicals. This also would include fixed fire protection systems like sprinklers, water spray, or deluge systems, monitor guns, dikes, designed drainage systems, and other systems to control or mitigate hazardous chemicals once an unwanted release occurs.

Written Procedures

The first step of an effective mechanical integrity program is to compile and categorize a list of process equipment and instrumentation to include in the program. This list includes pressure vessels, storage tanks, process piping, relief and vent systems, fire protection system components, emergency shutdown systems and alarms, and interlocks and pumps. For the categorization of instrumentation and the listed equipment, the employer should set priorities for which pieces of equipment require closer scrutiny than others.

Inspection and Testing

The mean time to failure of various instrumentation and equipment parts would be known from the manufacturer's data or the employer's experience with the parts, which then influence inspection and testing frequency and associated procedures. Also, applicable codes and standards—such as the National Board Inspection Code, or those from the American Society for Testing and Materials, American Petroleum Institute, National Fire Protection Association, American National Standards Institute, American Society of Mechanical Engineers, and other groups—provide information to help establish an effective testing and inspection frequency, as well as appropriate methodologies.

The applicable codes and standards provide criteria for external inspections for such items as foundation and supports, anchor bolts, concrete or steel supports, guy wires, nozzles and sprinklers, pipe hangers, grounding connections, protective coatings and insulation, and external metal surfaces of piping and vessels. These codes and standards also provide information on methodologies for internal inspection and a frequency formula based on the corrosion rate of the materials of construction. Also, internal and external erosion must be considered along with corrosion effects for piping and valves. Where the corrosion rate is not known, a maximum inspection frequency is recommended (methods of developing the corrosion rate are available in the codes). Internal inspections need to cover items such as the vessel shell, bottom and head; metallic linings; nonmetallic linings; thickness measurements for vessels and piping; inspection for erosion, corrosion, cracking and bulges; internal equipment like trays, baffles, sensors and screens for erosion, corrosion or cracking and other deficiencies. Some of these inspections may be performed by state or local government inspectors under state and local statutes. However, each employer must develop procedures to ensure that tests and inspections are conducted properly and that consistency is maintained even where different employees may be involved. Appropriate training must be provided to maintenance personnel to ensure that they understand the preventive maintenance program procedures, safe practices, and the proper use and application of special equipment or unique tools that may be required. This training is part of the overall training program called for in the standard.

Quality Assurance

A quality assurance system helps ensure the use of proper materials of construction, the proper fabrication and inspection procedures, and appropriate installation procedures that recognize field installation concerns. The quality assurance program is an essential part of the mechanical integrity program and will help maintain the primary and secondary lines of defense designed into the process to prevent unwanted chemical releases or to control or mitigate a release. "As built" drawings, together with certifications of coded vessels and other equipment and materials of construction, must be verified and retained in the quality assurance documentation.

Equipment installation jobs need to be properly inspected in the field for use of proper materials and procedures and to ensure that qualified craft workers do the job. The use of appropriate gaskets, packing, bolts, valves, lubricants and welding rods needs to be verified in the field. Also, procedures for installing safety devices need to be verified, such as the torque on the bolts on rupture disc installations, uniform torque on flange bolts, and proper installation of pump seals. If the quality of parts is a problem, it may be appropriate for the employer to conduct audits of the equipment supplier's facilities to better ensure proper purchases of required equipment suitable for intended service. Any changes in equipment that may become necessary will need to be reviewed for management of change procedures.

Nonroutine Work Authorizations

Nonroutine work conducted in process areas must be controlled by the employer in a consistent manner. The hazards identified involving the work to be accomplished must be communicated to those doing the work and to those operating personnel whose work could affect the safety of the process. A work authorization notice or permit must follow a procedure that describes the steps the maintenance supervisor, contractor representative, or other person needs to follow to obtain the necessary clearance to start the job. The work authorization procedures must reference and coordinate, as applicable, lockout/tagout procedures, line breaking procedures, confined space entry procedures, and hot work authorizations. This procedure also must provide clear steps to follow once the job is completed to provide closure for those that need to know the job is now completed and that equipment can be returned to normal.

Managing Change

To properly manage changes to process chemicals, technology, equipment and facilities, one must define what is meant by change. In the process safety management standard, change includes all modifications to equipment, procedures, raw materials, and processing conditions other than "replacement in kind." These changes must be properly managed by identifying and reviewing them prior to implementing them. For example, the operating procedures contain the operating parameters (pressure limits, temperature ranges, flow rates, etc.) and the importance of operating within these limits. While the operator must have the flexibility to maintain safe operation within the established parameters, any operation outside of these parameters requires review and approval by a written management of change procedure. Management of change also covers changes in process technology and changes to equipment and instrumentation. Changes in process technology can result from changes in production rates, raw materials, experimentation, equipment unavailability, new equipment, new product development, change in catalysts, and changes in operating conditions to improve yield or quality. Equipment changes can be in materials of construction, equipment specifications, piping pre-arrangements, experimental equipment, computer program revisions, and alarms and interlocks. Employers must establish means and methods to detect both technical and mechanical changes.

Temporary changes have caused a number of catastrophes over the years, and employers must establish ways to detect both temporary, and permanent changes. It is important that a time limit for temporary changes be established and monitored since otherwise, without control, these changes may tend to become permanent. Temporary changes are subject to the management of change provisions. In addition, the management of change procedures are used to ensure that the equipment and procedures are returned to their original or designed conditions at the end of the temporary change. Proper documentation and review of these changes are invaluable in ensuring that safety and health considerations are incorporated into operating procedures and processes. Employers may wish to develop a form or clearance sheet to facilitate the processing of changes through the management of change procedures. A typical change form may include a description and the purpose of the change, the technical basis for the change, safety and health considerations, documentation of changes for the operating procedures, maintenance procedures, inspection and testing, P&IDs, electrical classification, training and communications, pre-startup inspection, duration (if a temporary change), approvals, and authorization. Where the impact of the change is minor and well understood, a check list reviewed by an authorized person, with proper communication to others who are affected, may suffice. (See Figure 2 for a sample request for change form that can be helpful in guiding this procedure.)

For a more complex or significant design change, however, a hazard evaluation procedure with approvals by operations, maintenance, and safety departments may be appropriate. Changes in documents such as P&IDs, raw materials, operating procedures, mechanical integrity programs, and electrical classifications should be noted so that these revisions can be made permanent when the drawings and procedure manuals are updated. Copies of process changes must be kept in an accessible location to ensure that design changes are available to operating personnel as well as to PHA team members when a PHA is being prepared or being updated.

Incident Investigation

Incident investigation is the process of identifying the underlying causes of incidents and implementing steps to prevent similar events from occurring. The intent of an incident investigation is for employers to learn from past experiences and thus avoid repeating past mistakes. The incidents OSHA expects employers to recognize and to investigate are the types of events that resulted in or could reasonably have resulted in a catastrophic release. These events are sometimes referred to as "near misses," meaning that a serious consequence did not occur, but could have. (See Figure 3 for sample incident investigation report form.)

Employers must develop in-house capability to investigate incidents that occur in their facilities. A team should be assembled by the employer and trained in the techniques of investigation including how to conduct interviews of witnesses, assemble needed documentation, and write reports. A multi-disciplinary team is better able to gather the facts of the event and to analyze them and develop plausible scenarios as to what happened, and why. Team members

Figure 2

Notification of Process Change Checklist

Information about the Change:

Originator _____ Date of Origination _____

Proposed Date of Change _____ Area _____

☐ Permanent   ☐ Temporary   From _____ To _____

Description and Location of Change (Scope) _____

Technical Basis for Change _____

Nature of the Change:

Change affects: ☐ Safety   ☐ Loss Prevention   ☐ Environment   ☐ Health

Type of Change: ☐ Alarm   ☐ Shutdown Point   ☐ Addition or Removal of Equipment
                  ☐ Piping Modification ☐ Chemical   ☐ Process Computer Control
                  ☐ Job Procedure   ☐ Instrument   ☐ Equipment/Material Modification
                  ☐ Other_____

Premodification Checklist:

Applicable	NA	Initials	
☐	☐	_____	Consult piping and equipment specifications.
☐	☐	_____	Perform reactive chemicals testing. ☐ In process?
☐	☐	_____	Add involved materials to Toxic Substance Control Act (TSCA) inventory.
☐	☐	_____	Calculate impact on F&EI and CEI.
☐	☐	_____	Comply with Engineering Practices.
☐	☐	_____	Comply with Technology Center guidelines.
☐	☐	_____	Comply with Dow Environmental Protection Guideline for Operations.
☐	☐	_____	Comply with Safety and Loss Prevention requirements.
☐	☐	_____	Consult maintenance (name)_____.
☐	☐	_____	Consult instrument and electrical technician (name)_____.
☐	☐	_____	Consult parts technician (name)_____.
☐	☐	_____	Evaluate and modify relief system (name)_____.
☐	☐	_____	Consult Industrial Hygiene (name)_____.
☐	☐	_____	Consult Process Engineering (name)_____.
☐	☐	_____	Complete required reviews (name reviews)_____.
☐	☐	_____	Other_____.

Postmodification Checklist (Before Startup):

Applicable	N/A	Initials	
☐	☐	_____	Performed prestartup audit.
☐	☐	_____	Completed or updated training program.
☐	☐	_____	Wrote and obtained approval for job procedures.
☐	☐	_____	Updated P&IDs process flow sheets and plot plans.
☐	☐	_____	Trained personnel on the change.
☐	☐	_____	Updated critical instrument checklist.
☐	☐	_____	Changed computer code and documentation.

Approvals:

	Name	Date
Originator	_____	_____
First Reviewer	_____	_____
Department Head/Superintendent	_____	_____

Corporate S/LP/S
February 1992

Reprinted with permission of Dow Chemical USA,
2020 Dow Center, Midland, MI 48762.

Figure 3

National Safety Council

ACCIDENT INVESTIGATION REPORT

CASE NUMBER

COMPANY _____ ADDRESS _____

DEPARTMENT _____ LOCATION (if different from mailing address) _____

1. NAME of INJURED	2. SOCIAL SECURITY NUMBER	3. SEX ☐ M ☐ F	4. AGE	5. DATE of ACCIDENT

6. HOME ADDRESS	7. EMPLOYEE'S USUAL OCCUPATION	8. OCCUPATION at TIME of ACCIDENT

	9. LENGTH of EMPLOYMENT	10. TIME in OCCUP. at TIME of ACCIDENT
11. EMPLOYMENT CATEGORY	☐ Less than 1 mo. ☐ 6 mos. to 5 yrs.	☐ Less than 1 mo. ☐ 6 mos. to 5 yrs.
☐ Regular, full-time ☐ Temporary ☐ Nonemployee	☐ 1-5 mos. ☐ More than 5 yrs.	☐ 1-5 mos. ☐ More than 5 yrs.
☐ Regular, part-time ☐ Seasonal	12. CASE NUMBERS and NAMES of OTHERS INJURED in SAME ACCIDENT	
13. NATURE of INJURY and PART of BODY		

14. NAME and ADDRESS of PHYSICIAN	16. TIME of INJURY	17. SEVERITY of INJURY
	A. _____ A.M. P.M.	☐ Fatality
		☐ Lost workdays—days away from work
	B. Time within shift	☐ Lost workdays—days of restricted activity
15. NAME and ADDRESS of HOSPITAL		☐ Medical treatment
	C. Type of shift	☐ First aid
		☐ Other, specify _____

18. SPECIFIC LOCATION of ACCIDENT	19. PHASE OF EMPLOYEE's WORKDAY at TIME of INJURY
	☐ During rest period ☐ Entering or leaving plant
	☐ During meal period ☐ Performing work duties
ON EMPLOYER'S PREMISES? ☐ Yes ☐ No	☐ Working overtime ☐ Other _____

20. DESCRIBE HOW the ACCIDENT OCCURRED

_____

_____

_____

_____

_____

21. ACCIDENT SEQUENCE. Describe in reverse order of occurrence events preceding the injury and accident. Starting with the injury and moving backward in time, reconstruct the sequence of events that led to the injury.

A. Injury Event _____

B. Accident Event _____

C. Preceding Event #1 _____

D. Preceding Event #2, #3, etc _____

_____

Figure 3 (Continued)

22. TASK and ACTIVITY at TIME of ACCIDENT

A. General type of task _____

B. Specific activity _____

C. Employee was working:

☐ Alone ☐ With crew or fellow worker ☐ Other, specify _____

23. POSTURE of EMPLOYEE

_____

24. SUPERVISION at TIME of ACCIDENT

☐ Directly supervised ☐ Not supervised

☐ Indirectly supervised ☐ Supervision not feasible

25. CAUSAL FACTORS. Events and conditions that contributed to the accident. Include those identified by use of the Guide for Identifying Causal Factors and Corrective Actions.

_____

_____

_____

_____

_____

_____

_____

_____

_____

_____

26. CORRECTIVE ACTIONS. Those that have been, or will be, taken to prevent recurrence. Include those indentified by use of the Guide for Identifying Causal Factors and Corrective Actions.

_____

_____

_____

_____

_____

_____

_____

_____

_____

_____

PREPARED BY _____

TITLE _____

DEPARTMENT_____ DATE _____

APPROVED _____

TITLE _____ DATE _____

APPROVED _____

TITLE _____ DATE _____

should be selected on the basis of their training, knowledge, and ability to contribute to a team effort to fully investigate the incident.

Employees in the process area where the incident occurred should be consulted, interviewed or made a member of the team. Their knowledge of the events represents a significant set of facts about the incident that occurred. The report, its findings, and recommendations should be shared with those who can benefit from the information. The cooperation of employees is essential to an effective incident investigation. The focus of the investigation should be to obtain facts and not to place blame. The team and the investigative process should clearly deal with all involved individuals in a fair, open, and consistent manner.

Emergency Preparedness

Each employer must address what actions employees are to take when there is an unwanted release of highly hazardous chemicals. Emergency preparedness is the employer's third line of defense that will be relied on along with the second line of defense, which is to control the release of chemicals. Control releases and emergency preparedness will take place when the first line of defense to operate and maintain the process and contain the chemicals fails to stop the release. In preparing for an emergency chemical release, employers will need to decide the following:

- Whether they want employees to handle and stop small or minor incidental releases;

- Whether they wish to mobilize the available resources at the plant and have them brought to bear on a more significant release;

- Whether employers want their employees to evacuate the danger area and promptly escape to a preplanned safe zone area, and then allow the local community emergency response organizations to handle the release; or

- Whether the employer wants to use some combination of these actions.

Employers will need to select how many different emergency preparedness or third lines of defense they plan to have, develop the necessary emergency plans and procedures, appropriately train employees in their emergency duties and responsibilities, and then implement these lines of defense.

Employers, at a minimum, must have an emergency action plan that will facilitate the prompt evacuation of employees when there is an unwanted release of a highly hazardous chemical. This means that the employer's plan will be activated by an alarm system to alert employees when to evacuate, and that employees who are physically impaired will have the necessary support and assistance to get them to a safe zone. The intent of these requirements is to alert and move employees quickly to a safe zone. Delaying alarms or confusing alarms are to be avoided. The use of process control centers or buildings as safe areas is discouraged. Recent catastrophes indicate that lives are lost in these structures because of their location and because they are not necessarily designed to withstand over-pressures from shock waves resulting from explosions in the process area.

When there are unwanted incidental releases of highly hazardous chemicals in the process area, the employer must inform employees of the actions/procedures to take. If the employer wants employees to evacuate the area, then the emergency action plan will be activated. For outdoor processes, where wind direction is important for selecting the safe route to a refuge area, the employers should place a wind direction indicator, such as a wind sock or pennant, at the highest point visible throughout the process area. Employees can move upwind of the release to gain safe access to a refuge area by knowing the wind direction.

If the employer wants specific employees in the release area to control or stop the minor emergency or incidental release, these actions must be planned in advance and procedures developed and implemented. Handling incidental releases for minor emergencies in the process area must include pre-planning, providing appropriate equipment for the hazards, and conducting training for those employees who will perform the emergency work before they respond to handle an actual release. The employer's training program, including the Hazard Communication standard training, is to address, identify, and meet the training needs for employees who are expected to handle incidental or minor releases.

Preplanning for more serious releases is an important element in the employer's line of defense. When a serious release of a highly hazardous chemical occurs, the employer, through preplanning, will have determined in advance what actions employees are to take. The evacuation of the immediate release area and other areas, as necessary, would be accomplished under the emergency action plan. If the employer wishes to use plant personnel—such as a fire brigade, spill control team, a hazardous materials team—or employees to render aid to those in the immediate release area and to control or mitigate the incident, refer to OSHA's Hazardous Waste

Operations and Emergency Response (HAZWOPER) standard (Title 29 CFR Part 1910.120). If outside assistance is necessary, such as through mutual aid agreements between employers and local government emergency response organizations, these emergency responders are also covered by HAZWOPER. The safety and health protection required for emergency responders is the responsibility of their employers and of the on-scene incident commander.

Responders may be working under very hazardous conditions; therefore, the objective is to have them competently led by an on-scene incident commander and the commander's staff, properly equipped to do their assigned work safely, and fully trained to carry out their duties safely before they respond to an emergency. Drills, training exercises, or simulations with the local community emergency response planners and responder organizations is one means to obtain better preparedness. This close cooperation and coordination between plant and local community emergency preparedness managers also will aid the employer in complying with the Environmental Protection Agency's Risk Management Plan criteria.[1]

An effective way for medium to large facilities to enhance coordination and communication during emergencies within the plant and with local community organizations is by establishing and equipping an emergency control center. The emergency control center should be located in a safe zone so that it could be occupied throughout the duration of an emergency. The center should serve as the major communications link between the on-scene incident commander and plant or corporate management as well as with local community officials. The communications equipment in the emergency control center should include a network to receive and transmit information by telephone, radio, or other means. It is important to have a backup communications network in case of power failure or if one communication means fails. The center also should be equipped with the plant layout; community maps; utility drawings, including water for fire extinguishing; emergency lighting; appropriate reference materials such as a government agency notification list, company personnel phone list, SARA Title III reports and material safety data sheets, emergency plans and procedures manual; a listing with the location of emergency response equipment and mutual aid information; and access to meteorological data and any dispersion modeling data.

---

[1]EPA is required by the Clean Air Act Amendments of 1990 to develop regulations that will require companies to make available to the public information on the way the companies manage the risks of the chemicals they handle. These regulations will be developed in 1992. The OSHA PSM standard, which meets similar Clean Air Amendment requirements and the forthcoming EPA rules, will apply only to specified chemicals in listed quantities. OSHA and EPA's lists will not necessarily be identical.

Compliance Audits

An audit is a technique used to gather sufficient facts and information, including statistical information, to verify compliance with standards. Employers must select a trained individual or assemble a trained team to audit the process safety management system and program. A small process or plant may need only one knowledgeable person to conduct an audit. The audit includes an evaluation of the design and effectiveness of the process safety management system and a field inspection of the safety and health conditions and practices to verify that the employer's systems are effectively implemented. The audit should be conducted or led by a person knowledgeable in audit techniques who is impartial towards the facility or area being audited. The essential elements of an audit program include planning, staffing, conducting the audit, evaluating hazards and deficiences and taking corrective action, performing a follow-up and documenting actions taken.

Planning

Planning is essential to the success of the auditing process. During planning, auditors should select a sufficient number of processes to give a high degree of confidence that the audit reflects the overall level of compliance with the standard. Each employer must establish the format, staffing, scheduling, and verification methods before conducting the audit. The format should be designed to provide the lead auditor with a procedure or checklist that details the requirements of each section of the standard. The names of the audit team members should be listed as part of the format as well. The checklist, if properly designed, could serve as the verification sheet that provides the auditor with the necessary information to expedite the review of the program and ensure that all requirements of the standard are met. This verification sheet format could also identify those elements that will require an evaluation or a response to correct deficiencies. This sheet also could be used for developing the follow-up and documentation requirements.

Staffing

The selection of effective audit team members is critical to the success of the program. Team members should be chosen for their experience, knowledge, and training and should be familiar with the processes and auditing techniques, practices, and procedures. The size of the team will vary depending on the size and complexity of the process under consideration. For a large, complex, highly instrumented plant, it may be desirable to have team members with expertise in process engineering and design; process chemistry; instrumentation and computer controls; electrical hazards and classifications; safety and health disciplines; maintenance; emergency preparedness; warehousing or shipping; and process safety auditing. The team may use part-time members to provide the expertise required and to compare what is actually done or followed with the written PSM program.

Conducting the Audit

An effective audit includes a review of the relevant documentation and process safety information, inspection of the physical facilities, and interviews with all levels of plant personnel. Utilizing the audit procedure and checklist developed in the preplanning stage, the audit team can systematically analyze compliance with the provisions of the standard and any other corporate policies that are relevant. For example, the audit team will review all aspects of the training program as part of the overall audit. The team will review the written training program for adequacy of content, frequency of training, effectiveness of training in terms of its goals and objectives as well as to how it fits into meeting the standard's requirements. Through interviews, the team can determine employees' knowledge and awareness of the safety procedures, duties, rules, and emergency response assignments. During the inspection, the team can observe actual practices such as safety and health policies, procedures, and work authorization practices. This approach enables the team to identify deficiencies and determine where corrective actions or improvements are necessary.

Evaluation and Corrective Action

The audit team, through its systematic analysis, should document areas that require corrective action as well as where the process safety management system is effective. This provides a record of the audit procedures and findings and serves as a baseline of operation data for future audits. It will assist in determining changes or trends in future audits.

Corrective action is one of the most important parts of the audit and includes identifying deficiencies, and planning, following-up, and documenting the corrections. The corrective action process normally begins with a management review of the audit findings. The purpose of this review is to determine what actions are appropriate, and to establish priorities, timetables, resource allocations and requirements, and responsibilities. In some cases, corrective action may involve a simple change in procedures or a minor maintenance effort to remedy the problem. Management of change procedures need to be used, as appropriate, even for a seemingly minor change. Many of the deficiencies can be acted on promptly, while some may require engineering studies or more detailed review of actual procedures and practices. There may be instances where no action is necessary; this is a valid response to an audit finding. All actions taken, including an explanation when no action is taken on a finding, need to be documented.

The employer must assure that each deficiency identified is addressed, the corrective action to be taken is noted, and the responsible audit person or team is properly documented. To control the corrective action process, the employer should consider the use of a tracking system. This tracking system might include periodic status reports shared with affected levels of management, specific reports such as completion of an engineering study, and a final implementation report to provide closure for audit findings that have been through management of change, if appropriate, and then shared with affected employees and management. This type of tracking system provides the employer with the status of the corrective action. It also provides the documentation required to verify that appropriate corrective actions were taken on deficiencies identified in the audit.

Conclusion

OSHA believes the preceding discussion of PSM should help small employers to comply more easily with the new requirements the standard imposes. The end result can only be safer more healthful workplace for all employees—a goal we all share.

Appendix - Methods of Process Hazards Analysis

On July 17, 1990, OSHA issued a proposed rule for the management of hazards associated with processes using highly hazardous chemicals. This rule, called the Process Safety Management standard, was finalized on February 24, 1992.
In an appendix to the proposed rule, OSHA discussed several methods of process hazard analysis. That discussion, which may be helpful for those doing job hazard analyses, follows:

What-if. For relatively uncomplicated processes, review the process from raw materials to product. At each handling or processing step, "what if" questions are formulated and answered, to evaluate the effects of component failures or procedural errors on the process.

Checklist. For more complex processes, the "what if" study can be best organized through the use of a "checklist," and assigning certain aspects of the process to the committee members having the greatest experience or skill in evaluating those aspects. Operator practices and job knowledge are audited in the field, the suitability of equipment and materials of construction is studied, the chemistry of the process and the control systems are reviewed, and the operating and maintenance records are audited. Generally, a checklist evaluation of a process precedes use of the more sophisticated methods described below, unless the process has been operated safely for many years and has been subjected to periodic and thorough safety inspections and audits.

What-If/Checklist. The what-if/checklist is a broadly based hazard assessment technique that combines the creative thinking of a selected team of specialists with the methodical focus of a prepared checklist. The result is a comprehensive hazard analysis that is extremely useful in training operating personnel on the hazards of the particular operation.

The review team is selected to represent a wide range of production, mechanical, technical, and safety disciplines. Each person is given a basic information package regarding the operation to be studied. This package typically includes information on hazards of materials, process technology, procedures, equipment design, instrumentation control, incident experience, and previous hazards reviews. A field tour of the operation also is conducted at this time.

The review team methodically examines the operation from receipt of raw materials to delivery of the finished product to the customer's site. At each step, the group collectively generates a listing of "what-if" questions regarding the hazards and safety of the operation.

When the review team has completed listing its spontaneously generated questions, it systematically goes through a prepared checklist to stimulate additional questions.

Subsequently, answers are developed for each question. The review team then works to achieve a consensus on each question and answer. From these answers, a listing of recommendations is developed specifying the need for additional action or study. The recommendations, along with the list of questions and answers, become the key elements of the hazard assessment report.

Hazard and Operability Study (HAZOP). HAZOP is a formally structured method of systematically investigating each element of a system for all of the ways in which important parameters can deviate from the intended design conditions to create hazards and operability problems. The hazard and operability problems are typically determined by a study of the piping and instrument diagrams (or plant model) by a team of personnel who critically analyze effects of potential problems arising in each pipeline and each vessel of the operation.

Pertinent parameters are selected, for example, flow, temperature, pressure, and time. Then the effect of deviations from design conditions of each parameter is examined. A list of key words, for example, "more of," "less of," "part of," are selected for use in describing each potential deviation.

The system is evaluated as designed and with deviations noted. All causes of failure are identified. Existing safeguards and protection are identified. An assessment is made weighing the consequences, causes, and protection requirements involved.

Failure Mode and Effect Analysis (FMEA). The FMEA is a methodical study of component failures. This review starts with a diagram of the operation, and includes all components that could fail and conceivably affect the safety of the operation. Typical examples are instrument transmitters, controllers, valves, pumps, rotometers, etc. These components are listed on a data tabulation sheet and individually analyzed for the following:

• Potential mode of failure, (i.e., open, closed, on, off, leaks, etc);

• Consequence of the failure; effect on other components and effects on whole system;

• Hazard class, (i.e., high, moderate, low);

- Probability of failure;

- Detection methods; and

- Remarks/compensating provisions.

Multiple concurrent failures also are included in the analysis. The last step in the analysis is to analyze the data for each component or multiple component failure and develop a series of recommendations appropriate to risk management.

Fault Tree Analysis. A fault tree analysis can be either a qualitative or a quantitative model of all the undesirable outcomes, such as a toxic gas release or explosion, that could result from a specific initiating event. It begins with a graphic representation (using logic symbols) of all possible sequences of events that could result in an incident. The resulting diagram looks like a tree with many branches listing the sequential events (failures) for different independent paths to the top event. Probabilities (using failure rate data) are assigned to each event and then used to calculate the probability of occurrence of the undesired event.

This technique is particularly useful in evaluating the effect of alternative actions on reducing the probability of occurrence of the undesired event.

States with Approved Plans

COMMISSIONER
Alaska Department of Labor
1111 West 8th Street
Room 306
Juneau, AK 99801
(907) 465-2700

DIRECTOR
Industrial Commission of Arizona
800 W. Washington
Phoenix, AZ 85007
(602) 542-5795

DIRECTOR
California Department
 of Industrial Relations
455 Golden Gate Avenue
4th Floor
San Francisco, CA 94102
(415) 703-4590

COMMISSIONER
Connecticut Department of Labor
200 Folly Brook Boulevard
Wethersfield, CT 06109
(203) 566-5123

DIRECTOR
Hawaii Department of Labor
 and Industrial Relations
830 Punchbowl Street
Honolulu, HI 96813
(808) 586-8844

COMMISSIONER
Indiana Department of Labor
State Office Building
402 West Washington Street
Room W195
Indianapolis, IN 46204
(317) 232-2378

COMMISSIONER
Iowa Division of Labor Services
1000 E. Grand Avenue
Des Moines, IA 50319
(515) 281-3447

SECRETARY
Kentucky Labor Cabinet
1049 U.S. Highway, 127 South
Frankfort, KY 40601
(502) 564-3070

COMMISSIONER
Maryland Division of Labor
 and Industry
Department of Licensing
 and Regulation
501 St. Paul Place, 2nd Floor
Baltimore, MD 21202-2272
(410) 333-4179

DIRECTOR
Michigan Department of Labor
Victor Office Center
201 N. Washington Square
P.O. Box 30015
Lansing, MI 48933
(517) 373-9600

DIRECTOR
Michigan Department
 of Public Health
3423 North Logan Street
Box 30195
Lansing, MI 48909
(517) 335-8022

COMMISSIONER
Minnesota Department of Labor
 and Industry
443 Lafayette Road
St. Paul, MN 55155
(612) 296-2342

DIRECTOR
Nevada Department of Industrial
 Relations
Capitol Complex
1370 S. Curry Street
Carson City, NV 89710
(702) 687-3032

SECRETARY
New Mexico Environmental
 Department
Occupational Health
 and Safety Bureau
1190 St. Francis Drive
P.O. Box 26110
Santa Fe, NM 87502
(505) 827-2850

COMMISSIONER
New York Department of Labor
State Office Building - Campus
12
Room 457
Albany, NY 12240
(518) 457-2741

COMMISSIONER
North Carolina Department
 of Labor
4 West Edenton Street
Raleigh, NC 27601
(919) 733-0360

ADMINISTRATOR
Department of Consumer
 and Business Services
Labor and Industries Building
350 Winter Street, NE, Room 430
Salem, OR 97310
(503) 378-3272

SECRETARY
Puerto Rico Department of Labor
 and Human Resources
Prudencio Rivera Martinez
Building
505 Munoz Rivera Avenue
Hato Rey, PR 00918
(809) 754-2119

COMMISSIONER
South Carolina Department
 of Labor
3600 Forest Drive
P.O. Box 11329
Columbia, SC 29211-1329
(803) 734-9594

COMMISSIONER
Tennessee Department of Labor
710 James Robertson Parkway
Suite "A" - 2nd Floor
Nashville, TN 37243-0659
(615) 741-2582

COMMISSIONER
Industrial Commission of Utah
P.O. Box 146600
Salt Lake City, UT 84110-6600
(801) 530-6898

COMMISSIONER
Vermont Department of Labor
 and Industry
120 State Street
Montpelier, VT 05620
(802) 828-2288

COMMISSIONER
Virgin Islands Department
 of Labor
2131 Hospital Street
Christiansted
St. Croix, VI 00840-4666
(809) 773-1994

COMMISSIONER
Virginia Department of Labor
 and Industry
Powers-Taylor Building
13 South 13th Street
Richmond, VA 23219
(804) 786-2377

DIRECTOR
Washington Department of Labor
 and Industries
General Administration Building
P.O. Box 44001
Olympia, WA 98504-4001
(206) 956-4213

ADMINISTRATOR
Occupational Safety and Health
 Administration
Herschler Building, 2nd Floor
East
122 West 25th Street
Cheyenne, WY 82002
(307) 777-7672

OSHA Consultation Project Directory

State	Telephone
Alabama	(205) 348-3033
Alaska	(907) 269-4939
Arizona	(602) 542-5795
Arkansas	(501) 682-4522
California	(415) 703-4441
Colorado	(303) 491-6151
Connecticut	(203) 566-4550
Delaware	(302) 577-3908
District of Columbia	(202) 576-6339
Florida	(904) 488-3044
Georgia	(404) 894-8274
Guam	(671) 647-4202
Hawaii	(808) 586-9116
Idaho	(208) 385-3283
Illinois	(312) 814-2337
Indiana	(317) 232-2688
Iowa	(515) 281-5352
Kansas	(913) 296-4386
Kentucky	(502) 564-6895
Louisiana	(504) 342-9601
Maine	(207) 624-6460
Maryland	(410) 333-4218
Massachusetts	(617) 969-7177
Michigan	(517) 322-8250(H)
	(517) 322-1809(S)
Minnesota	(612) 297-2393
Mississippi	(601) 987-3981
Missouri	(314) 751-3403
Montana	(406) 444-6418
Nebraska	(402) 471-4717

Nevada	(702) 486-5016
New Hampshire	(603) 271-2024
New Jersey	(609) 292-3923
New Mexico	(505) 827-2877
New York	(518) 457-2481
North Carolina	(919) 733-2360
North Dakota	(701) 221-5188
Ohio	(614) 644-2631
Oklahoma	(405) 528-1500
Oregon	(503) 378-3272
Pennsylvania	(412) 357-2396
Puerto Rico	(809) 754-2171
Rhode Island	(401) 277-2438
South Carolina	(803) 734-9599
South Dakota	(605) 688-4101
Tennessee	(615) 741-7036
Texas	(512) 440-3834
Utah	(801) 530-6868
Vermont	(802) 828-2765
Virginia	(804) 786-8707
Virgin Islands	(809) 772-1315
Washington	(206) 956-5443
West Virginia	(304) 558-7890
Wisconsin	(608) 266-8579(H)
	(608) 266-1818(S)
Wyoming	(307) 777-7786

(H) - Health
(S) - Safety

OSHA Area Offices

Area	Telephone
Albany, NY	(518) 464-6742
Albuquerque, NM	(505) 766-3411
Allentown, PA	(215) 776-0592
Anchorage, AK	(907) 271-5152
Appleton, WI	(414) 734-4521
Augusta, ME	(207) 622-8417
Austin, TX	(512) 482-5783
Avenel, NJ	(908) 750-3270
Baltimore, MD	(410) 962-2840
Baton Rouge, LA	(504) 389-0474
Bayside, NY	(718) 279-9060
Bellevue, WA	(206) 553-7520
Billings, MT	(406) 657-6649
Birmingham, AL	(205) 731-1534
Bismarck, ND	(701) 250-4521
Boise, ID	(208) 334-1867
Bowmansville, NY	(716) 684-3891
Braintree, MA	(617) 565-6924
Bridgeport, CT	(203) 579-5579
Calumet City, IL	(708) 891-3800
Carson City, NV	(702) 885-6963
Charleston, WV	(304) 347-5937
Cincinnati, OH	(513) 841-4132
Cleveland, OH	(216) 522-3818
Columbia, SC	(803) 765-5904
Columbus, OH	(614) 469-5582
Concord, NH	(603) 225-1629
Corpus Christi, TX	(512) 888-3257
Dallas, TX	(214) 320-2400
Denver, CO	(303) 844-5285
Des Plaines, IL	(708) 803-4800

Des Moines, IA	(515) 284-4794
Englewood, CO	(303) 843-4500
Erie, PA	(814) 833-5758
Fort Lauderdale, FL	(305) 424-0242
Fort Worth, TX	(817) 885-7025
Frankfort, KY	(502) 227-7024
Harrisburg, PA	(717) 782-3902
Hartford, CT	(203) 240-3152
Hasbrouck Heights, NJ	(201) 288-1700
Hato Rey, PR	(809) 766-5457
Honolulu, HI	(808) 541-2685
Houston, TX	(713) 286-0583
Houston, TX	(713) 591-2438
Indianapolis, IN	(317) 226-7290
Jackson, MS	(601) 965-4606
Jacksonville, FL	(904) 232-2895
Kansas City, MO	(816) 426-2756
Lansing, MI	(517) 377-1892
Little Rock, AR	(501) 324-6291
Lubbock, TX	(806) 743-7681
Madison, WI	(608) 264-5388
Marlton, NJ	(609) 757-5181
Methuen, MA	(617) 565-8110
Milwaukee, WI	(414) 297-3315
Minneapolis, MN	(612) 348-1994
Mobile, AL	(205) 441-6131
Nashville, TN	(615) 781-5423
New York, NY	(212) 264-9840
Norfolk, VA	(804) 441-3820
North Aurora, IL	(708) 896-8700
Oklahoma City, OK	(405) 231-5351
Omaha, NE	(402) 221-3182
Parsippany, NJ	(201) 263-1003
Peoria, IL	(309) 671-7033
Philadelphia, PA	(215) 597-4955

Phoenix, AZ .... (602) 640-2007

Pittsburgh, PA .... (412) 644-2903

Portland, OR .... (503) 326-2251

Providence, RI .... (401) 528-4669

Raleigh, NC .... (919) 856-4770

Salt Lake City, UT .... (801) 524-5080

San Francisco, CA .... (415) 744-7120

Savannah, GA .... (912) 652-4393

Smyrna, GA .... (404) 984-8700

Springfield, MA .... (413) 785-0123

St. Louis, MO .... (314) 425-4249

Syracuse, NY .... (315) 451-0808

Tampa, FL .... (813) 626-1177

Tarrytown, NY .... (914) 682-6151

Toledo, OH .... (419) 259-7542

Tucker, GA .... (404) 493-6644

Westbury, NY .... (516) 334-3344

Wichita, KS .... (316) 269-6644

Wilkes-Barre, PA .... (717) 826-6538

Related Publications

OSHA-2056 *All About OSHA*

OSHA-3084 *Chemical Hazard Communication*

OSHA-3047 *Consultation Services for the Employer*

OSHA-3088 *How to Prepare for Workplace Emergencies*

OSHA-2098 *OSHA Inspections*

OSHA-3021 *OSHA: Employee Workplace Rights*

OSHA-3077 *Personal Protective Equipment*

OSHA-3132 *Process Safety Management*

OSHA-3079 *Respiratory Protection*

Hazard Communication Standard, Title 29, Code of Federal Regulations (CFR) Part 1910.1200.

Process Safety Management of Highly Hazardous Chemicals Standard, Title 29, Code of Federal Regulations (CFR) Part 1910.119 FR 57, P. 6356. This contains the actual text of the PSM rule.

(A single free copy of the above materials can be obtained from OSHA Publications Office, Room N3101, Washington, DC 20210, (202) 523-9667).

OSHA-3104 Hazard Communication - A Compliance Kit
(A reference guide to step-by-step requirements for compliance with the OSHA standard.)

OSHA-3071 *Job Hazard Analysis*

(OSHA 3104 and OSHA 3071 are available from the Superintendent of Documents, U.S. Government Printing Office, Washington, DC 20402, (202) 783-3238. OSHA 3104 - GPO Order No. 929-022-000009, $18-domestic; $22.50-foreign. OSHA 3071 - GPO Order No. 029-016-00142-5, $1.00.)